MW00592483

PLAY WINNING TENNIS

with Perfect Strategy

Book 4

Julio Yacub

Illustrations by Henche Silberstein

Playing Winning Tennis with Perfect Strategy, Book 4

Copyright © 2008 Julio Yacub. All rights reserved. No part of this book may be reproduced or retransmitted in any form or by any means without the written permission of the publisher.

Published by Wheatmark™
610 East Delano Street, Suite 104, Tucson, Arizona 85705 U.S.A.
www.wheatmark.com

ISBN: 978-1-60494-051-0
LCCN: 2008921661

PREFACE

As a self-taught tennis player, I always looked for books that could help me improve my game. Most of the books that I read were long, wordy, and complicated. In college, I had the same problem: books, books, books, but none to my taste, simple but in-depth. I always needed to make outlines to focus on the specific things I wanted to work on. It is true that a good way of learning is to make your own outline, but sometimes we need them ready in order to concentrate on the goals without getting lost in words. This book is written in outline form, and it is simple to follow. You can even take it down to the court and concentrate on any stroke simply by taking a glimpse at that specific page.

Play Winning Tennis with Perfect Strategy is designed for visual learners and students of the game who look for simplicity without cutting corners, but it is not picture-perfect. In this ever-changing game, where there are many stances, several ways to take the racquet back, hit the ball, and follow through, it would be impossible for me to include everything. That's why I laid out this book as a guide, so you can understand how biomechanics work in tennis, and, with the help of your local pro, I hope you can improve your tennis game dramatically.

Even though the drawings and diagrams are shown from a right-handed player's perspective, any left-handed player can interpret them by using a mirror image view. I included side and front views for most of the strokes so the conversion would be easier. Also, to better understand the court diagrams, place yourself in it or imagine that you are on the court playing that particular pattern (instead of just thinking player A and player B). Finally, when using the terms "he" and "his," I imply, by all means, "she" and "hers."

Julio Yacub

ACKNOWLEDGMENT

I must mention that without the help of many people I would not be the person and player that I am today. I would like to thank my mentors, Nick Bollettieri, Vic Braden, and Dennis Van Der Meer, for their continuous contributions to the game and my tennis life.

A special thanks to Jack Groppel and Jim Loehr, who enlightened me to the realms of sport psychology and biomechanics (when they talk...I listen!). I would also like to extend my warmest gratitude to my first coach Ron Steele, former head coach of the Israeli Davis Cup team, for taking me under his wing when I was nothing. Thanks to the USTA High Performance Coaching Program team, especially to Nick Saviano and Paul Lubbers, for raising the stakes in American coaching. Sincere appreciation to my friends John Lapham and Claudio Yamus...and to all my students for sticking with me all these years...you have been the source of my inspiration.

Finally, and most importantly, I would like to thank my family, especially my wife Maura and my mother Henche Silberstein, without whose contributions and support this book would be just a fantasy.

This book belongs to the instructional tennis series "Play Winning Tennis," which covers every aspect of the complete competitive player.

- Book 1: *Playing Winning Tennis with Perfect Fundamentals*
- Book 2: *Playing Winning Tennis with Perfect Basic Strokes*
- Book 3: *Playing Winning Tennis with Perfect Specialty Shots*
- Book 4: *Playing Winning Tennis with Perfect Strategy*
- Book 5: *If I Play Better Tennis, Why Can't I Win?*

LEGEND

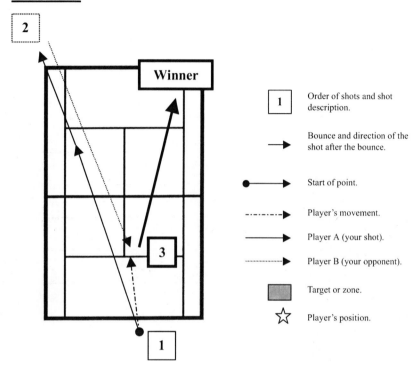

1	Order of shots and shot description.
➤	Bounce and direction of the shot after the bounce.
●——➤	Start of point.
-·-·-·-·➤	Player's movement.
———➤	Player A (your shot).
·········➤	Player B (your opponent).
▨	Target or zone.
☆	Player's position.

NOTE:

- All diagrams are shown from a right-handed player's perspective, and, unless mentioned, all patterns are identical from the ad or deuce courts, consequently, easily convertible for left-handed players as well as for planning a strategy from both courts. (Patterns are based on geometry of the court and percentage, not player's strength or weakness).

- All "order of shots and shot description" boxes are border coded with the respective shot (line) for easy recognition.

BOOK 4: PLAY WINNING TENNIS

WITH PERFECT STRATEGY

PERFECT STRATEGY

BASIC STROKES

STRATEGY: PLAYING THE GAME

Basic Strategy, Winning Patterns and Percentage Tennis

GENERAL RULE:

KEEP THE BALL IN THE COURT

- Hit the ball as hard as you can, as long as you can keep it in the court, for the duration of the point. You must find the limit of your power (how hard you can hit) before losing control of the ball.
- Control is the key to consistency, and spin will be the means to achieve it.[1]
- Once you can keep the ball in play consistently (long rallies), you'll need to be able to direct the ball and follow a high percentage winning pattern (strategy) and/or follow a specific plan (tactic) to exploit your opponent's weaknesses.

Keeping the Ball in Play

- Play within the gray box (mostly with topspin), leaving a safety path of 3 feet around it, to achieve fewer unforced errors, greater continuity of shots, and, thereby, keeping the ball in the court.

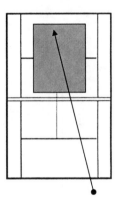

Shot Selection

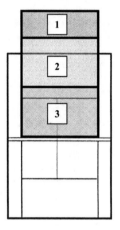

Tennis is about situations and executions. The best tennis happens when it is played on automatic pilot. In order to achieve this, use an automatic shot selection according to the situation. Remember, there is no right or wrong. Each situation can have several variables, so it is a matter of judgment, position and opportunity.

1. If you are in this box (**1**) just before making contact, play *defensive shots* (usually high and deep).
2. If you are in this box (**2**) just before making contact, play *percentage shots* (build up the point and create an opportunity to finish the point).
3. If you are in this box (**3**) just before making contact, play *offensive shots*, which include: transitional shots, volleys, and overheads (finish the point).

<u>GROUNDSTROKES</u>: Forehand and Backhand

1. KEEP THE BALL CROSSCOURT

- Do you ever wonder why professionals keep crosscourt rallies longer than any other kind of rallies? They know that the first one who changes direction takes a greater risk by hitting a lower percentage shot (i.e. down the line). That is why the player who has more consistent crosscourt shots will probably end up winning the game.

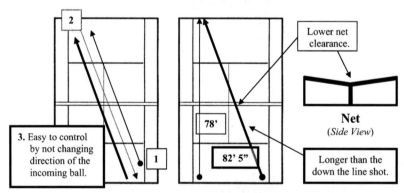

Easy to Control **Length and Height of the Shot**

12

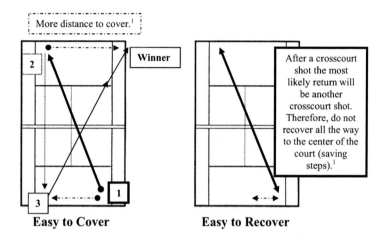

Easy to Cover   **Easy to Recover**

2. WHEN TO HIT DOWN THE LINE

- Hit down the line mostly for attacking shots.
- On short balls, like approach shots, follow to the net.
- After sharp angle shots, hit outside in, behind the player.

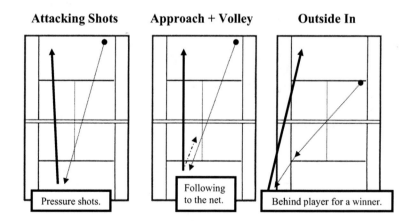

Attacking Shots   **Approach + Volley**   **Outside In**

13

3. HIT DEEP

- If you lose your rhythm or timing and find yourself missing shots, get out of trouble by hitting deep (and high). Your opponent will not be able to attack, and this will give you enough hitting time to get back into rhythm. For players who move well side to side, hit deep and right at the body.

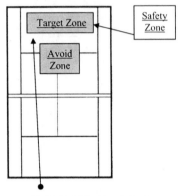

4. USE YOUR STRENGTH (Exploit Opponent's Weaknesses)

- For most of the players, a forehand is not just a shot but a weapon. This shot, when used properly, can open up the court or force a weak return. One good example is running around the backhand and hitting an inside-out shot. Your strength might be some other shot. Find it and use it wisely.

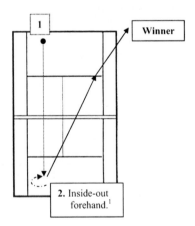

14

- Change strategy when your opponent's weakness is stronger than your weakness.

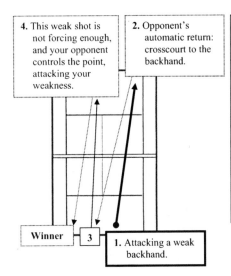

4. This weak shot is not forcing enough, and your opponent controls the point, attacking your weakness.

2. Opponent's automatic return: crosscourt to the backhand.

Be aware when you attack a weakness. Make sure that your opponent's return is not an automatic shot to your weakness, especially if your weakness is weaker than your opponent's. This situation will create an advantage in his favor and make it very difficult for you to follow your plan. The example shown to the left is one of many combinations, which depends on your and your opponent's shot-making abilities.

Winner | 3

1. Attacking a weak backhand.

5. MOVE YOUR OPPONENT

- Move your opponent side to side, forcing him into a defensive game (also opening the court for angle shots).
- Wrong footing your opponent by hitting behind him (especially on clay courts, where changing directions is most difficult).

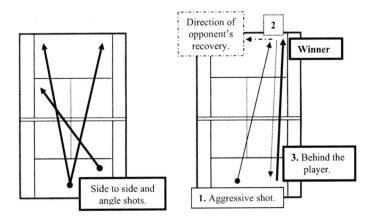

Side to side and angle shots.

Direction of opponent's recovery. | 2

Winner

3. Behind the player.

1. Aggressive shot.

15

6. FORCING GROUNDSTROKES: Attacking Game
(Imposing a Weak Return by Utilizing your Strength and Strategy)

- **Powerful shots** (hard and heavy spin). To be used in conjunction with a well-rounded tactical plan, especially to a weakness, forcing a mistake or a weak return to open up the court or go for a winner.
- **Tactical shots**. Be smart on the court and exploit your opponent's weaknesses, maximizing you strength. Use ball placement, spin, and power to win the important points.[1]
- **Pressure shots**. By keeping the pressure with high percentage tennis and depth throughout the rally (also by charging the net), you can make your opponent become impatient, and he may go for difficult or low percentage shots.
- **Hitting early**. By stepping inside the baseline and making contact early (at peak of the bounce), cutting off time for your opponent to react.

MAJOR POINTS TO CONSIDER

- To win you do not necessarily need better strokes than your opponent. Play percentage tennis and always follow a good strategic plan, maximizing your strength and attacking your opponent's weaknesses.
- Be flexible enough to change your game plan in order to adapt to your opponent's counter-attack (momentum shifts).
- *Good shot selection*: know your limitations. Do not attack when you are out of position. When under pressure, return the shot deep to a weakness (lob or looping shot), regain good position in the court, and return to your plan.
- If your opponent hits hard, powerful, deep groundstrokes move back a little (to gain time), but if he hits a lot of angle shots, you should move inside the baseline in order to cut off the angle of the shot more easily.
- In difficult moments always analyze the situation and reach a decision for the next strategy.
- Keep unforced errors to a minimum by not changing the direction of the incoming ball (when you are under pressure, return shots to the same location that the ball came from).
- Apply good topspin on baseline rallies, and aim 3 feet inside the lines.
- Keep the pressure on by following the serve with an aggressive forcing shot (first shot right after the serve).

VOLLEY

1. **FIRST VOLLEY** (After the approach shot or any transitional shot.)
   - Do not try to win this shot. This volley is a difficult one (far from net, out of position), and should be treated as a *set up shot*.
   - As your opponent is about to return your transitional shot, you should be at the "Ideal Split Area" (ISA) doing a split step.[2] With a split at the right time (right before your opponent contacts the ball), you should be able to reach the first volley. Then keep moving forward to the "Ideal Volley Area" (IVA), split again to place a more effective volley, maybe even a winner (closer to the net).

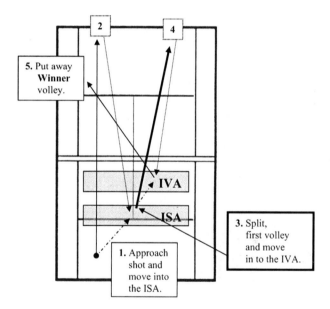

- There are endless combinations between the first volley and subsequent volleys (put away shots), but placing the first volley deep and straight ahead (of your position), will not create a sharp angle, and therefore, will make it much easier to cover the net (check also "High and Low" volleys).
- Do not get too close to the net, otherwise, any lob will become unreachable.
- Notice that after the split step you should move *diagonally* forward.[2] This way, as you move to the ball, you get closer to the net, cutting off the angle

17

of any possible shot. By doing this, you gain angle production for your volley, you attack the ball aggressively, and you shorten the reaction time of your opponent.

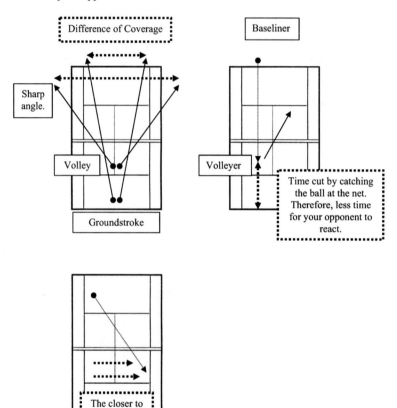

Where to Stand Once You Get to the "Ideal Volley Area" (IVA)

- Always stay in front of your opponent's eyes, wherever he is on the court (at the baseline or coming up to the net, covering any possible angle).

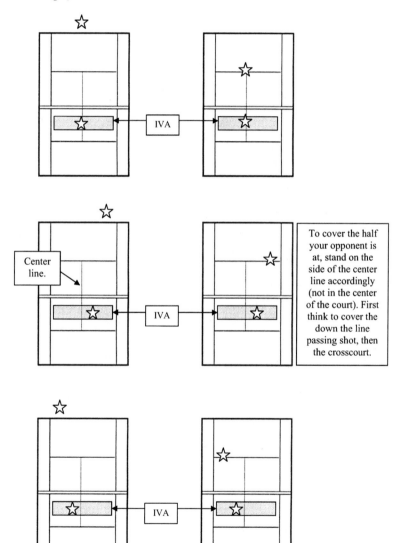

To cover the half your opponent is at, stand on the side of the center line accordingly (not in the center of the court). First think to cover the down the line passing shot, then the crosscourt.

2. LOW VOLLEY

- On low volleys or when volleying close to the sideline, aim *deep* down the line. This way, by not creating an angle, it will be easier to cover the next volley. Also, when volleying a low shot, you will need to open slightly the face of the racquet (how much will depend on your position relative to the net and how deep you need the shot to be), which will produce a higher bouncing shot. If this volley lands short, your opponent will move up, attacking you and putting away the easy shot. Hitting that low shot crosscourt instead will open up the court creating too much net to cover.

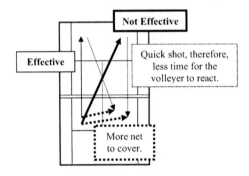

3. HIGH VOLLEY

- On high volleys, when at the "Ideal Volley Area", hit crosscourt or away from the player for an aggressive shot or winner put away.

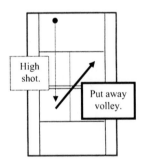

SERVE

1. PLACING THE FIRST SERVE into the Forehand

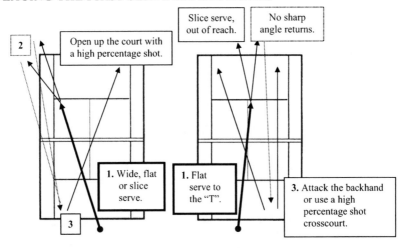

Slice serve, out of reach.

No sharp angle returns.

2

Open up the court with a high percentage shot.

1. Wide, flat or slice serve.

1. Flat serve to the "T".

3. Attack the backhand or use a high percentage shot crosscourt.

3

PLACING THE FIRST SERVE into the Backhand

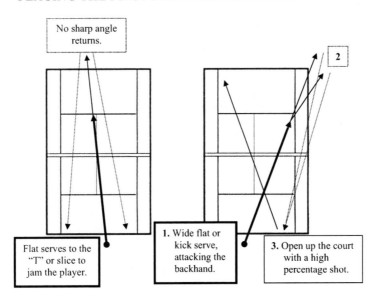

No sharp angle returns.

2

Flat serves to the "T" or slice to jam the player.

1. Wide flat or kick serve, attacking the backhand.

3. Open up the court with a high percentage shot.

21

2. PLACING THE SECOND SERVE

Same strategy as that of the first serve, but:

- Use more spin and kick serves for higher percentage shots.[3]
- Attack a weakness.
- Mix up the serves (placement and spin) to keep your opponent guessing, so your opponent will not have the chance to attack a weaker second serve.
- Aim deep, but not as deep as a first serve.
- If second serve is weak, make sure you get more first serves in, taking some pace off and replacing it with spin (higher percentage serve).

SERVE VARIATIONS (First and Second)

Right to the Body

Usually flat, but most effective when mixed up with different spins.

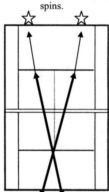

Wide Angle

Usually shorter, with slice to the deuce court and topspin to the ad court.

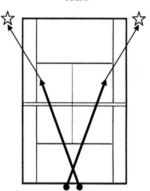

SERVER'S GOALS

Hold the Service Game

- Get between 60 to 70 percent of first serves in.
- Get the first serve in on important points.[2]
- Impose an offensive (aggressive) game in order to follow the strategy planned (disregarding player's game style). Also, force for a weak return so you can start the attack right from the first shot after the serve.

RETURN OF SERVE

- Depth and placement should be the focus, not power.
- For fast serves, use a block style return. If possible, depending on reaction time, serve speed, and spin, apply some topspin.
- On weak serves, attack the ball and follow to the net.
- For placement, think strategy: your strength against his weakness.

1. WHERE TO STAND FOR A *FIRST* SERVE
- If the serve is fast and deep, stand about 1 to 3 feet behind the baseline to gain some time and produce a solid return. Also consider shortening up the backswing and holding the racquet an inch or two shorter (especially for long body racquets) to be able to maneuver more quickly.
- If the serve is usually wide, especially with slice, stand closer to the baseline to cut down the angle of the serve and move diagonally to the ball.[2]
- Consider all variables: spins, depth, wind and surface of the court.

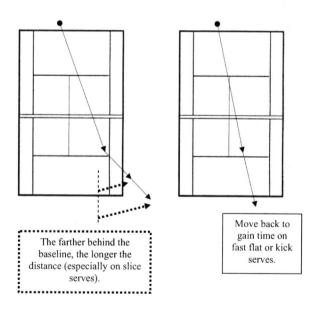

The farther behind the baseline, the longer the distance (especially on slice serves).

Move back to gain time on fast flat or kick serves.

23

2. WHERE TO STAND FOR A *WEAK OR SECOND* SERVE

- If the serve is weak, move inside the baseline. Consider the "Chip & Charge" strategy.
- For second serves stand closer to the baseline to keep up the pressure on the server and to get ready to attack the shorter serve.

3. RETURNING A *WIDE* SERVE

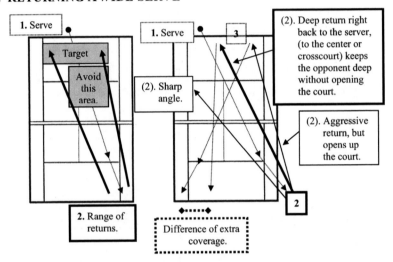

4. RETURNING A *DOWN THE T* SERVE

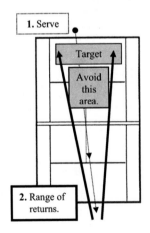

5. RETURNING A *"RIGHT TO THE BODY"* SERVE

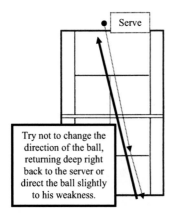

Try not to change the direction of the ball, returning deep right back to the server or direct the ball slightly to his weakness.

6. RETURNING A *"SERVE & VOLLEY"* PLAYER
 - **When the Serve is *Wide***

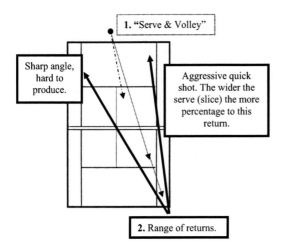

1. "Serve & Volley"

Sharp angle, hard to produce.

Aggressive quick shot. The wider the serve (slice) the more percentage to this return.

2. Range of returns.

- **When the Serve is *Down the "T"***

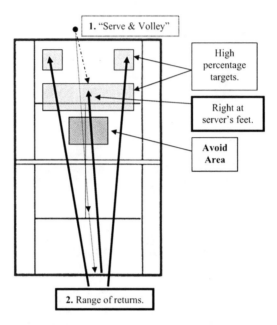

7. RETURNING AND ATTACKING THE NET ("Chip & Charge")
(Shallow and Second Serves)

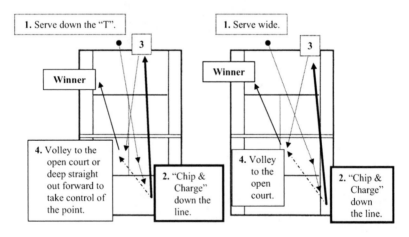

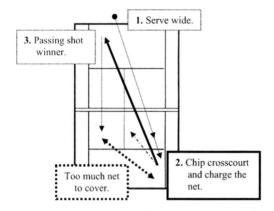

- Returning crosscourt when charging the net leaves too much net to cover (low percentage). If the plan is attacking a weak forehand or backhand, the crosscourt could be the right choice, but for most cases a better shot would be deep down the center towards the weak side, reducing the distance between you and the next possible shot.

RETURNER'S GOALS

Break Service Game
- Anticipate the serve by watching the toss position, spin and racquet face at point of contact.[3]
- Return the ball at all costs, regardless of how strong your opponent's serve is.
- Impose your game, aiming deep to a weakness or by using a specific pattern of play, forcing the server to make a weak shot.
- Get to the net ("Chip & Charge") whenever possible.

Note: When not mentioned, examples for the deuce court (forehand) will be identical for the ad court (backhand).

OVERHEAD

- When the overhead is hit off the center of the court, the most effective target is the opposite area close to the intersection of the service line and the singles sideline because this produces the most pronounced angle, which makes it impossible to return. It is a harder target to hit, so a deep shot to the open court will also do the job.

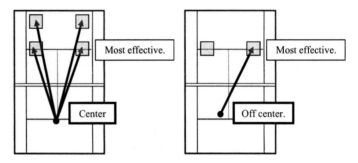

- Always try to hit overheads without the bounce, rather than letting the ball bounce (cuts off the opponent's time to recover). Also if you let it bounce, the angle of incidence will make this bouncing overhead difficult to hit, moving you further back away from the net and reducing your aggressive position.
- Let the ball bounce on very high lobs. Those super high lobs are tough to judge and the angle of incidence will not be an issue.

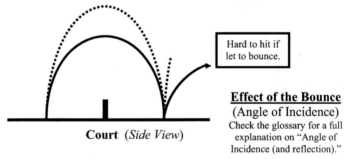

Court (*Side View*)

Hard to hit if let to bounce.

Effect of the Bounce
(Angle of Incidence)
Check the glossary for a full explanation on "Angle of Incidence (and reflection)."

[1] See book 1, chapter **"Anticipation & Footwork"**
[2] See chapter **"While Playing the Match"**
[3] See book 1, chapter **"Spins"**

PERFECT STRATEGY

TRANSITIONAL GAME

APPROACH SHOT

HALF VOLLEY

TRANSITIONAL SHOTS:

APPROACH SHOT, SWINGING VOLLEY, HALF VOLLEY

- The weaker you are as a volleyer *or* the greater you opponent's passing shots are, the better your transitional shots ought to be.

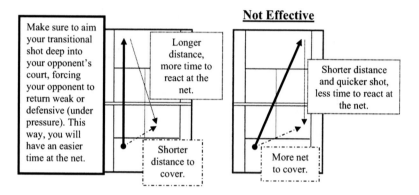

Not Effective

Make sure to aim your transitional shot deep into your opponent's court, forcing your opponent to return weak or defensive (under pressure). This way, you will have an easier time at the net.

Longer distance, more time to react at the net.

Shorter distance to cover.

Shorter distance and quicker shot, less time to react at the net.

More net to cover.

- *Note*: A short transitional shot will leave too much time for your opponent to react and attack you (you might still be in a vulnerable position), and therefore, finding a way to pass you.
- **Range of Motion**
  Aiming the approach shot *straight ahead* of your position in the court (down the line for off center shots), will lead you into a much easier position to cover any possible passing shot from your opponent.

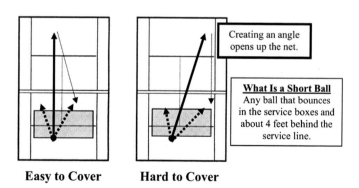

Creating an angle opens up the net.

What Is a Short Ball
Any ball that bounces in the service boxes and about 4 feet behind the service line.

Easy to Cover   **Hard to Cover**

31

SERVE & VOLLEY

1. FIRST SERVE

- A forcing serve is a must. With a second serve the surprise effect and psychological factor will not be as effective as with the first serve.
- Deep kick serves will give more time to reach the net and will keep your opponent behind the baseline due to the high bounce.
- Place serve tactically, exploiting the opponent's weaknesses.

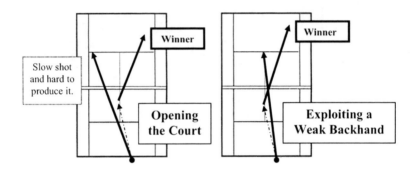

2. FIRST VOLLEY
Covering the Net

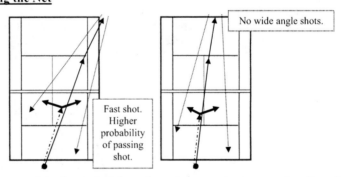

- Placement of the first volley depends on the serve placement and quality of the opponent's return. Sometimes your best volley is to the open court (make him move) or behind your opponent (opposite to his motion). However, most importantly, keep the opponent guessing.

SPECIALTY SHOTS

LOB

- Defensive or offensive, the lob is not an easy shot to perform. Take into consideration the height of the player, his ability to move, the quality of his overheads, the sun and wind conditions.
- Usually it is played high to the backhand side, so the opponent will have a hard time returning a high bouncing backhand shot (it is much harder than a high forehand shot), and crosscourt, because the court is longer (higher percentage shot).

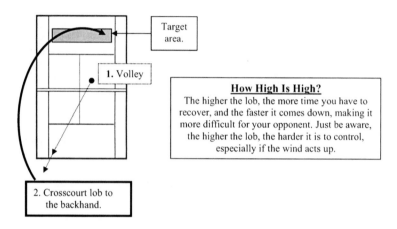

Target area.

1. Volley

How High Is High?
The higher the lob, the more time you have to recover, and the faster it comes down, making it more difficult for your opponent. Just be aware, the higher the lob, the harder it is to control, especially if the wind acts up.

2. Crosscourt lob to the backhand.

WHEN TO USE THE LOB
Defensive and Offensive

- In pressure situations (deep behind baseline and under aggressive attack) and when time to recover is required (regaining court positioning).
- Physical tiredness and to slow down the pace of the point.
- Against a good volleyer.
- Against a volleyer who gets too close to the net (between 4 to 6 feet from the net).
- Against a quick net rusher (especially if he does not do a split step).[2]
- To charge the net and become offensive (element of surprise).
- When the sun is in you opponent's eyes.
- When your opponent moves slowly or lacks a good overhead.

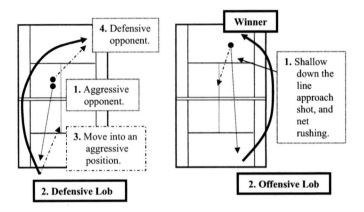

DROP SHOT

- Do not use the drop shot on critical points (15-40).
- Do not overuse it! It works better with the element of surprise (and well disguised).
- Most effective on slower courts (red clay or green "Har-Tru"), and especially when your opponent is well behind the baseline and you are inside the baseline.
- A good drop shot should bounce 3 times in the service box.
- Use it to change pace on a point or to change your opponent's rhythm.
- A very efficient combination against a slower or poorly conditioned player is to make a drop shot and then lob over his head. Also, the drop shot is effective against players who run around the backhand, hitting inside-out forehands, but not aggressively enough (shallow shots).
- Always move up after making a drop shot (covering any possible shot, like another drop shot from your opponent).

How to Read a Drop Shot
- Your opponent holds the forward motion of the racquet (before point of contact) too long.
- Your opponent opens the racquet face as point of contact is executed.
- Anticipate the drop shot by realizing your position (well behind the baseline) with your opponent's position (well inside the court).

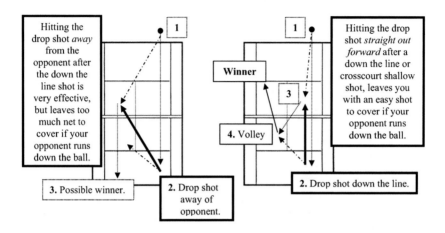

PASSING SHOT

- Placement of the passing shot depends on your position, your opponent's transitional shot placement, and his position in the court. Also, consider your ability to produce a hard shot under pressure and your opponent's ability to move at the net.
- Best passing shots are struck early with authority (at peak of bounce) and low over the net (flat or with heavy topspin).
- Always the quickest is the down the line passing shot. Because the ball covers less distance, the volleyer has less time to react.
- The crosscourt passing shot has a higher percentage of clearance over the net due to crossing over the lowest part of the net (center) and creates less court to cover on any possible opponent's volley.
- When the opponent comes up the middle of the court, a quick low shot into the shoelaces will cut down the probabilities of an angle shot, and, most likely, he will volley up, leaving you to deal with an easy high passing shot.
- Another possibility when the opponent is in a good tactical position (center of reach for your possible passing shot) is to aim directly at him with a powerful drive.

Covering After the Passing Shot

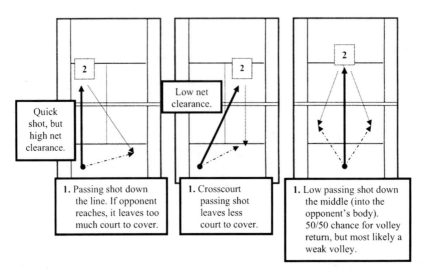

Quick shot, but high net clearance.

Low net clearance.

1. Passing shot down the line. If opponent reaches, it leaves too much court to cover.

1. Crosscourt passing shot leaves less court to cover.

1. Low passing shot down the middle (into the opponent's body). 50/50 chance for volley return, but most likely a weak volley.

When Hitting a *Cross Court* Passing Shot

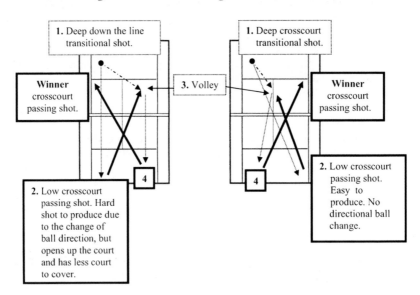

1. Deep down the line transitional shot.

1. Deep crosscourt transitional shot.

Winner crosscourt passing shot.

3. Volley

Winner crosscourt passing shot.

2. Low crosscourt passing shot. Hard shot to produce due to the change of ball direction, but opens up the court and has less court to cover.

2. Low crosscourt passing shot. Easy to produce. No directional ball change.

When Hitting a *Down the Line* Passing Shot

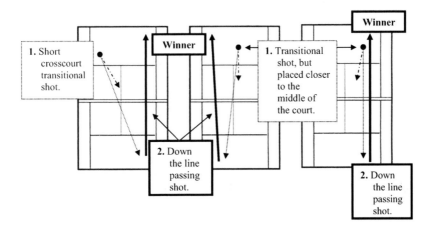

- A *shallow* transitional shot or volley should be attacked down the line (or to the open court), going for a winner or a forcing volley.
- A *deep* transitional shot can also be attacked down the line, but this shot must be selected when the opponent is hesitating, running late (far from net) and/or recovering to the center of the "Ideal Split Area" too quickly, miss-timing the split step.[2]
- Any transitional shot (or net player) can be neutralized with a defensive or offensive lob depending on the situation (player position, player moving forward too fast, and ability to move back).
- Never change your mind when aiming the passing shot, just go for it and force your opponent into a weak volley.

PASSING SHOT VARIATION

ANGLE PASSING SHOT

- A low percentage shot! Choose the right time to perform it.
- Use extreme topspin to hit the target areas and go for a clean winner (spin is the main source of energy. Any extra speed or power on the ball will lower the chance for success).
- Always cover for any possible return.

39

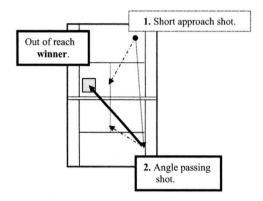

ANGLE SHOT

- You opponent must hit a short, wide, close to the sideline shot to produce a sharp angle shot.
- You must use extreme topspin to hit the target areas and go for a clean winner.
- Make sure your opponent is off position or behind the baseline when using this shot.
- Always cover for any possible return.

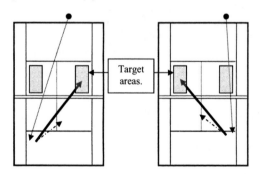

Difference Between a Deep Crosscourt and an Angle Shot

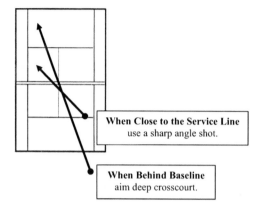

When Close to the Service Line
use a sharp angle shot.

When Behind Baseline
aim deep crosscourt.

---

[1] See book 1, chapter **"Spins"**
[2] See book 1, chapter **"Anticipation & Footwork"**

PLAYING THE ELEMENTS

PLAYING THE ELEMENTS

WIND

Playing on windy days is much harder than in normal conditions; but if you include the wind in your tactics, the wind will become a new weapon.

- Shorten up the swings to compensate for the wind factor on the ball.
- Do not make big risky shots by aiming close to the lines.
- Be patient and use high percentage shots.
- Realize how strong the wind is and from which direction the wind blows so you can adjust to it properly.
- Make good footwork a priority to adjust for the wind factor.
- Play high percentage *first* serves. Wind has more effect on spinning second serves.

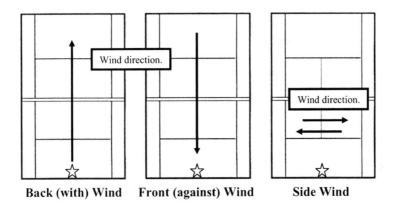

| Back (with) Wind | Front (against) Wind | Side Wind |

Playing with *Back Wind*

- Wind blows from behind you, carrying the ball deeper, therefore, hit *lower and shorter* than normal.
- Use more topspin on all strokes.
- Attack the net and use the volleys more frequently (a good passing shot gets attenuated by the opponent's front wind).
- Use defensive slice lobs, but consider that the wind will carry that ball deeper than where you are aiming.

Playing with *Front Wind*
- Wind blows against you, slowing down the ball. Therefore, hit *higher and deeper* than normal.
- When long rallies are played and you get tired (since playing *against* the wind requires more energy expenditure than playing *with* the wind), use more angle shots and come to the net to finish up the point quicker.
- Use flatter and harder groundstrokes and serves.
- Use drop shots.
- Use slice with caution (can get short and, therefore, invite your opponent to attack you).
- Use offensive topspin lobs.

Playing with *Side Wind*
- Wind blows from either side across the court.
- Do not aim close to the sideline. Adjust your aiming according to the wind factor.
- Use spin to control the flight of the ball.
- When using a slice serve, measure the wind factor.

SUN
- Use moon-balls and lobs more often when the sun is in front of your opponent's eyes.
- When moon-balls and lobs are used against you, use your free hand to block the sun.
- Adjust toss and stance when serving into the sun.
- "Serve & Volley" only as a surprise element when playing against the sun.

WEATHER AND OTHER CONDITIONS

When playing in different environment (altitude, humidity, indoor, outdoor), acclimatization can take from 4 to 14 days for the body to adapt.

Heat and Humidity
- Humidity limits the effectiveness of body's sweating mechanism. Therefore, consider a lot of fluid replacement.
- If perspiring profusely and playing for more than two hours on a hot day, consider a sport drink which can replace lost minerals and electrolytes (like magnesium, calcium, sodium, and potassium) to avoid muscle cramping.

- If your opponent is in better shape, conserve your energy by not trying to chase out-of-reach shots (usually you should go for everything, even those unreachable ones) or "Serve & Volley" frequently. Come to the net as soon as you can, mostly when your opponent hits a shallow shot. This will make the point shorter, saving you some energy. If your opponent hits deep, use the moon-shot to slow down the pace of the point, thereby, recovering physically (the ball spends more time in the air) and getting to a better position on the court.

Indoor/Outdoor
- Indoor lighting differs from direct sunlight.
- Indoor consistent environment contrasts with outdoor weather conditions.
- Different surfaces (some only indoor).[1]

Altitude
- The higher the altitude, the faster the speed of the ball.
- Greater tendency to hit long.
- Easy to get tired quicker due to difficulty of breathing at high altitude (oxygen load).

[1] See chapter **"Playing Different Surfaces"**

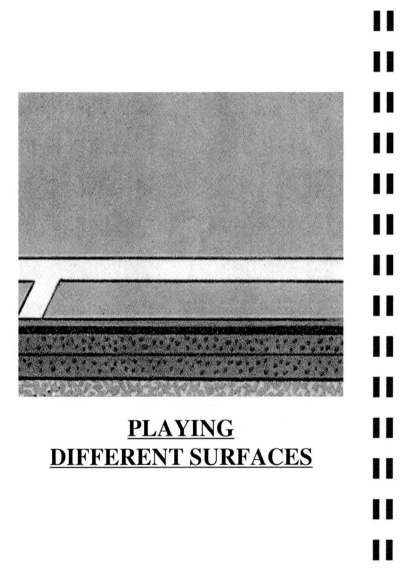

PLAYING
DIFFERENT SURFACES

PLAYING DIFFERENT SURFACES

GRASS COURTS
- Construction: very short and compact grass like at Wimblendon, England.
- Court speed: *fast* due to low and unpredictable bounces.
- Low traction, slippery.
- Low impact on knees.
- Strategy: "Serve & Volley" players will dominate the game on this surface. Also suitable for aggressive all court players with a powerful first serve. Quick short points should be the basics of strategy.

HARD COURTS
- Construction: asphalt or concrete usually coated with multiple layers of a mix of acrylic paint and sand.
- Court speed: *fast*. The less abrasive the surface, the faster the court is (the more sand in the mix, the more abrasive).
- Low to medium ball bounce. The smoother the surface, the lower the bounce (ball skids and stays low). Bounce is consistent but depends on surface smoothness and level.
- High impact surface, therefore, hard on knees (most of the impact is absorbed with your legs).
- Best surface for aggressive baseline (with an aggressive first serve), all-court, and "Serve & Volley" players.[1] Because each point happens so quickly, concentration should be a major concern for the player.

CUSHIONED COURTS
- Construction: asphalt or concrete topped with a firm cushioned carpet covered with acrylic and sand mix.
- Most common surfaces are Deco Turf II (US Open), Rebound Ace (Australian Open).
- Court speed: *medium to fast*. Speed of the bounce of the ball depends on abrasiveness of surface coat mixture.
- Medium ball bounce. The ball has more rebound than hard courts due to the resiliency of the cushioned carpet and the roughness of the topcoat. Bounce is more uniform than hard due to consistency of the cushioned layer.

51

- Easier on the knees than hard courts (the cushioned carpet absorbs some of the shock).
- Hard hitters ("Serve & Volley" players, consistent baseliners) and spin players will benefit from this surface, as well as players with explosive footwork and high level of concentration.

CARPET COURTS

- Construction: rubber-like synthetic or textile carpet on a base of asphalt or concrete.
- Mostly used in indoor courts.
- Court speed: *medium to fast*. Speed depends on material of the carpet. Some textiles are slower than hard. Some synthetics are faster than hard.
- Low to medium ball bounce. Ball tends to have a lower bounce than hard courts. Ball bounce is most consistent. Bad bounces will occur only on old carpets (mostly around the seams).
- Excellent traction. Clay court players will feel that the feet stick to the surface.
- Better than cushioned courts on your knees. Carpet absorbs most of the shock before it transfers up to your knees.
- Best suited for all-court, thinking players (strategy) due to the high consistency of the bounce. Spin is very effective due to the abrasiveness of the surface.

CLAY COURTS

- Construction: a layer of red clay or synthetic green clay is laid over a fine crushed stone base.
- Most common surface in country clubs (indoors and outdoors) in America (green "Har-Tru"). Very popular in Europe, like in the French Open, and South America (red clay).
- Court speed: *slow*. The ball speed is slowed down by the bite of the dust at the bounce.
- High ball bounce. Clay grabs into the ball fuzz and enhances the spin (topspin kicks high, drop shots stays low). Might have some bad bounces due to the surface imperfections from playing. Some shots hitting the lines might also have some unpredictability.
- Sliding footwork techniques are needed.
- Low impact on knees.

- Best suited for patient (expect long rallies), consistent aggressive baseline players and counter-punchers. Spin and depth should be the basics for strategy, as well as good movement, fitness level, and mental toughness.

[1] See chapter **"Different Players"**

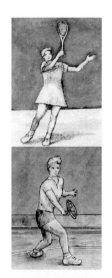

PLAYING
DIFFERENT PLAYERS

GAME STYLES: <u>DIFFERENT PLAYERS</u>

Knowing what type of player you are and identifying your opponent's game style will provide a foundation for your strategy in every particular match.

OFFENSIVE GAME (Aggressive Baseline Players, "All-Court" Players and "Serve & Volley" Players / Net Rushers)

Advantages:
- Backcourt aggressive shots, forcing for a weak return or a mistake.
- Aggressive inside out shots to create angle winners, weak opponent's shots, or openings.
- Approach shots put a lot of pressure on your opponent, rushing him into a difficult passing shot as he sees you approaching to the net.
- Volleys shorten up the point by reducing the baseliner reaction time and, therefore, putting your opponent under heavy strain. [1]
- Overheads are put away winners. If you attack the short balls and follow to the net, you have a chance to hit this shot (as well as volleys).
- Constantly changing spins, placement, and pace (drop shots, angle shots, etc.).
- Following a specific strategy or pattern of play, which maximizes your weapons (best shots, usually aggressive play).

Disadvantage:
- Riskier. If your rhythm is off, a defensive player could prevail.

THE AGGRESSIVE BASELINE PLAYER
- Most of the action happens from the baseline, attacking and dictating the point with spin and power.
- Fast and powerful groundstrokes.
- Usually these kinds of players are very quick and will get to any ball, adding pace and depth to the shot.
- Usually they have one strong weapon.

Counterattacking an Aggressive Baseliner

- Be patient and consistent, play more like a retriever with high percentage shots, and let the aggressive player make a mistake as he goes for shots.
- For deep aggressive shots, back up a couple of feet behind the baseline, and shorten up your backswings, feeding from his pace and gaining time.
- If you are more aggressive than your opponent, impose your strength first (dictate the point right from the first shot).
- Find a weakness (usually backhand), and take advantage of it.
- Run around the backhand when possible, but be selective.
- Mix up spins and take pace off the ball with slice shots.
- Come to the net every opportunity you get.
- Attack second serves. Put the aggressive baseliner under attack, forcing him into a defensive mode.
- Bring the aggressive baseliner to the net, lob over his head, and/or force him to volley.

THE "ALL-COURT" PLAYER

- Aggressive and defensive players without a major weapon but possessing an all-around game, who are not afraid to attack the net.
- Good fitness level players.

Counterattacking an "All-Court" Player

- Impose your strength right from the first shot.
- Use percentage tennis and solid game plans.[1]

THE "SERVE & VOLLEY" PLAYER / NET RUSHER

- Quick and agile players.
- Excellent net positioning and coverage.
- Excellent spin serves.

Counterattacking a "Serve & Volley" Player / Net Rusher

- Make sure you focus on the ball, not on the net rusher
- Serve effectively (power, spin, and placement) against a net rusher otherwise he will take command of the point.
- Do not rally with the volleyer. Try to win with one or two quick passing shots.

- Mix up returns, some with no pace and good placement (low into shoelaces), some hard right to the body, and mostly crosscourt (not extremely wide serves).[1]
- Use offensive lob whenever possible.

DEFENSIVE GAME (Retrievers)

Advantages:
- Backcourt steady game.
- Not taking any kind of risk (not attacking the short balls, therefore, no approach shots, no volleys, and no overheads).
- Following a retriever game plan, one more ball over the net. Might also have a specific strategy plan, but its execution and success will depend on the player's ability to control the ball.

Disadvantage:
- The defensive game lets your opponent use his weapons, and, therefore, the offensive player dictates and takes control of the point.

THE RETRIEVER (Counter-Puncher)
- Sometimes called pushers or human backboards. They love to stay at the baseline and return every ball back. They do not use a particular spin, pace or depth, but manage to get it back.
- Some better retrievers or counter-punchers will develop depth and spin, and effectively will use moon-balls (very high and deep topspin shots) as they react to their opponent's game.
- Very consistent, patient, and fit.

Counterattacking a Retriever
- Be patient. Prepare yourself for a long match.
- Do not start pushing the ball yourself; they are kings and queens in that department. Instead, find weaknesses (or a weaker shot) in his game and exploit them (imposing your strength).
- Get to the net on every opportunity you have, even on not so short balls, but be aware of moon-balls.
- Mix up spins and pace. Sometimes they feed from your power. Therefore, some weak shots combined with aggressive shots will take them out of their comfort zone. Also, bring them to the net and lob over their heads or hit some low shoelace shots.

- Focus on closing the point. If you are out of position just put the ball back and deep, as it is unlikely that a retriever will take advantage or your vulnerable position.

PREPARING
FOR A MATCH

PREPARING FOR A MATCH

STRENGTH TRAINING AND AEROBIC ENDURANCE

Though tennis is a control game, power plays a large role in success. The fitter the player, the longer high performance can be sustained, and, therefore, the higher the chance of accomplishing the task at hand.

Major tennis-specific muscles to consider for *strength training*:[1]
- Shoulder: Anterior, Middle, Posterior Deltoids
- Chest: Pectorals
- Stomach: Abdominals
- Back of Arm: Triceps
- Forearm: Flexors-Extensors
- Back and Lower Back: Latissimus Dorst and Eractors
- Sides: Obliques
- Thigh: Quadriceps
- Back of thigh: Hamstrings
- Calf: Gastrocnemius

For *aerobic endurance*, long-distance runs are ideal. Also, consider treadmills, steppers, bikes, etc.[1]

BALANCE AND AGILITY

Once the strokes are mastered (mechanically sound shots), tennis is mostly a game of strategy and footwork (lower-body). Therefore, quickness and agility are basic ingredients to an effective game, and because most of the shots are hit in motion, good balance is essential.

Balance Drills[1]
- Stand on one foot and maintain balance without wobbling.
- Run on a straight line.
- **Hexagon Drill**

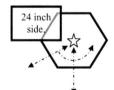

24 inch side

Standing inside the hexagon, jump over every panel to the outside, and back in immediately, in a counterclockwise direction.

63

Working on any kind of footwork and anaerobic exercises will benefit your ability to maintain balance, get more agile, and improve quickness.

Footwork Drills[1]

❖ Stress good rhythm and balance throughout the exercise.
- Shuffles: side-stepping.
- Carrioca steps: side-stepping with a cross step in front and one behind.
- High knee jog: jog raising the knees to waist high.
- Butt kick jog: jog kicking your butt with your heels.
- Plyometrics drills: speed and agility drills usually facilitated with cones, ladders, medicine balls, and elastic bands.

Anaerobic Drills[1]
Spider Drill

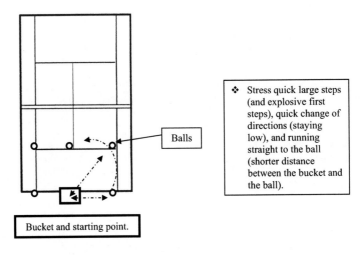

Balls

❖ Stress quick large steps (and explosive first steps), quick change of directions (staying low), and running straight to the ball (shorter distance between the bucket and the ball).

Bucket and starting point.

1. Place 5 balls and an empty bucket (or a racquet) on the intersections of the lines as shown above.
2. Pick up the balls one at a time, in consecutive order, in a counterclockwise direction, placing them into the bucket (or on your racquet instead). Average time for men and women is between 17 to 19 seconds.

Suicide Run

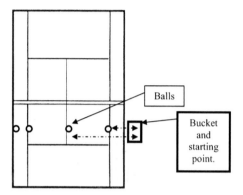

1. Place 4 balls and an empty bucket on the lines as shown above.
2. Pick up the balls one at a time, in consecutive order, placing them into the bucket. Average time for men and women is between 15 to 17 seconds.
❖ Stress explosive first steps and quick change of directions (staying low).

Shuffle, Sprint, Back-Pedal Drill

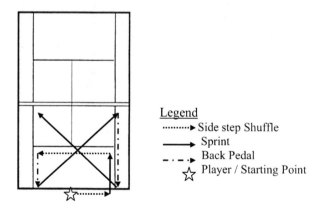

1. Follow the lines according to the legend (or make your own pattern).
❖ Stress balance (especially when backpedaling), speed, and rhythm.

KNOWING YOUR GAME

It is essential if you are to win that you know your strengths and weaknesses. Knowing your game will help you map a plan suited to your abilities. Once you identify a strength, work on it until becomes a weapon and then win points by maximizing it. By knowing your weaknesses you can try to work around them, planning a strategy that avoids them.

For an easy identification of your strengths and weaknesses, chart your shots, rate them and plan goals for future improvement.[2]

DATE_____

SHOT[3]	STRENGTH ┈┈▶ WEAKNESS										GOAL
	10	9	8	7	6	5	4	3	2	1	
Forehand											
Backhand											
Volley											
Serve											
Return of Serve											
Overhead											
Approach Shot											
Swinging Volley											
Half Volley											
Lob											
Drop Shot											
Passing Shot											
Angle Shot											
Footwork											
Fitness											
Mental Toughness											

[1] For exercises and specifics on this subject consult a qualified specialist.
[2] See *Charting Future goals* in chapter **"After the Match"**
[3] Include forehand and backhand sides for all strokes.

<u>BEFORE THE MATCH</u>

BEFORE THE MATCH

GET READY

- Make sure your equipment (racquets, strings, shoes, etc.) is in good condition.
- One to two hours before the match, eat low glycemic-index carbohydrates (maintains blood sugar level for a longer period) like bananas, oatmeal, yogurt, rice, and pasta. Also, include some vegetables and other fruits in your pre-match diet.
- Avoid foods with high sugar content prior to any exercise (due to a quick drop in blood sugar level).
- Have a good night's sleep.
- 30 minutes before the match drink about 250–350 ml. of fluids.

PRESET PLANS

- Preset plans help to build up confidence before the match. At the actual match it will be the foundation of your game. These plans must be refined and adjusted according to each opponent, as you discover his game as the match develops (tactics).
- Every player is different, but determine and practice your preset plans based on your strengths. For example:
  - **Plan A:** I will play aggressively from the baseline, controlling with the backhand and pressing with my forehand, and as soon as I get a short forehand, I will attack down the line and follow to the net.
  - **Plan B:** I will stay at the baseline, using extreme topspin, aiming deep to the center to minimize unforced errors.
  - **Plan C:** I will bring my opponent to the net, lob over his head, mix spins, use angle shots and drop shots.

PSYCHE UP

- Get hungry to win (desire), but do not let your adrenaline control you (high emotions), otherwise, that will interfere with your mental game (state of relaxation during the present moment of a point).
- Have confidence on yourself (expect to perform well, do not just hope to win).
- Use imagery to picture yourself winning points (and specific shots) during that particular match.
- Stay relaxed and positive, confident that you have preset plans to face the opponent (better if you already know your opponent).

PLAYING AUTOMATIC TENNIS
Entering and Staying in the "Zone"
Automatic tennis is a state of mind sometimes called playing in the "zone", where body and mind are linked together in complete harmony, turning the game into automatic reaction, where everything works and a feeling of total enjoyment reigns.

The key elements to enter and stay in the "zone" are:
- Have your mind relax (quiet) by having confidence on your strokes, Preset plans, and a good strategically understanding of the game.
- Use imagery (visualization) to build up more confidence, especially about winning patterns of play (using your strength).
- Disregard the opponent. Play the ball and use targets as you play the point.
- Avoid distractions by concentrating on the ball, especially at point of contact (yours and your opponent's).[1]
- Most important: *Enjoy the moment.*

INJURY PREVENTION[2]
Caution: Stretching without proper warm up (when muscles are cold) may increase chance of injury.

Tennis players require flexibility to play good tennis. Therefore, warm up and stretching becomes essential for all level of players. For injury prevention, **warm up** should be performed ritually *before* the workout and **stretching** *after* the workout (cool down).

Off Court Warm Up
Before hitting any tennis balls, raise your body temperature.
- Light jog around the court.
- Jump rope.
- Jog in place.

Once the body temperature has been raised, do warm up rotations to get the muscles ready for strenuous work.

- **Neck Rotation**
  Do not take the head back, just to the side and forward.

- **Shoulder Rotation**
  A. Arms on the side, make circles with the shoulders as wide as possible. Both directions.

B. Hands on shoulders, make wide forward rotations with the elbows and then go backwards.

C. Arms extended, shoulder level and palm down. First rotate arms in small slow circles, slowly increasing range and speed. Forward and backward. Repeat with palm up.

- **Hip Rotation**
  Hands on hips, rotate trunk without pulling back (to the side and forward). Both directions.

> **Variation**
> **Trunk and hip rotation** with hands behind the head.

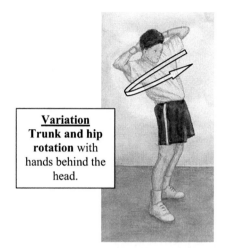

- **Trunk Rotation**
  Arms extended to the sides, shoulder level. Rotate trunk to one side and to the other side without lifting the feet (that will tell you how far you should go).

73

On Court Warm Up
Once a light sweat occurs (warmer muscles can elongate better without injure) start a tennis warm up.

Mini-Tennis
- 3-5 minutes. Mini-tennis is an excellent tool to warm up your strokes before hitting full court. However, sometimes before a match there is a 10 minute time limit, and, therefore, only full court warm up should be performed.
- Mini-tennis is played in the four service boxes, playing full strokes at 20% power.

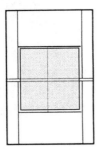

Variations of mini-tennis
Two boxes down the line (one in front of the other). Crosscourt (diagonal) backhands (left to right), and forehands (right to left).

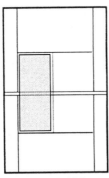
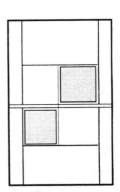

Down the Line   **Crosscourt**

Full Court
- Start at 50% power and slowly increase intensity.
- 5-10 minutes, (groundstrokes, volleys, overheads, and serves).

Major Points to Observe (Identifying Weaknesses)
While warming up, analyze your opponent's game (weaknesses and strengths) in order to plan your strategy.[3]
- Grounstroke preference (running around the backhand).
- Late point of contacts.
- Spins (forehand and backhand).
- Where most errors on groudstrokes occur, at the net or deep?
- Which stance he predominantly uses?
- Does he volley with one or two hands on the backhand side?
- Does he swing at the ball or have a compact punch?
- Does he slice on the overhead or have a flat put-away?
- Does he place the serve or just hit it?
- What kind of spin he controls on the serve (first and second).
- Does he change the toss position when changing spins?
- Is he left-handed or right-handed?

[1] See *Focus on the Ball* in chapter **"While Playing the Game"**
[2] See *Avoiding Injuries* in chapter **"After the Match"**
[3] See chapter **"Strategy"**

WHILE PLAYING
THE MATCH

WHILE PLAYING THE MATCH

Should You Serve First or Choose Side?
- If you have a good first serve choose to serve to get an early lead.
  Also, holding the first game carries a psychological advantage because the opponent must hold his game in order to stay in the game (tie).
- If your serve is good, but you feel off rhythm, choose side.
- If your return is better than your serve (and the serve is efficient), choose side. Break your opponent's serve, and then hold your service game. This way you secure the first two games of the set.

DURING THE POINT
- *Take control of the point*: play aggressively the first two shots of each point (serve and first shot, return of serve and subsequent shot).
- *Play automatic tennis*: do not think or talk to yourself while playing the point.
- *Feel relaxed*: enjoy the moment, especially the heat of competition (stay motivated to play, compete, learn, and improve). Let winning be an outcome of performance.
- *Reduce stress* by knowing what you are capable of doing as far as stroke production is concerned (know your game).
- *Maintain a positive attitude at all times*. Remember, confidence is an outcome of winning and performing. Therefore, staying positive and persistent through the matches will eventually help you to achieve results.
- *Play within your limits* (good shot selection) and calculate risky shots.

IN BETWEEN POINTS
Tennis is practically a game of emergencies and pressure. How you handle these situations and the pressure will determine success or defeat. In between points is the critical time to analyze and control all these factors, especially the emotional control, in order to be flexible enough to change or adapt to a new strategy if necessary.

Emotional Control and Adaptability
If a Point Is Won
- Pump up to keep energy high (yeah!, come on!).
- Physical recovery (use several slow deep breaths).
- Plan next point.

79

If a Point Is Lost

- *Emotional Recovery*
  The most common human reaction is to get down on oneself after losing a particular shot (easy or difficult shot to perform). This kind of behavior is only prejudicial to your performance. You feel bad about yourself, muscles get tight and footwork slows down, mind wanders over the last point and eye vision does not focus on the ball. Therefore, you have a poor performance on the following point. Losing a point is not easy, especially if you really try hard, but be subjective.
    - Do not get down on yourself. Whatever you say (mostly in one word or short sentence), stay positive, saying something that could help you for the following point (ok, keep the pressure, deep, I know what to do, come on!).
    - Think in the present time (next coming point), not the past (maybe just a quick rehearsal of the correct imaginary shot right after the mistake).
    - Analyze the situation and adapt a countering plan.

IMPORTANT POINTS
Game
- If opponent is not strong, get an early lead. Pay attention (play focused) to 30-love or 30-15 advantage. Winning the next point will leave you in a very advantageous position (and especially a psychological advantage).
- If opponent is about your level, play focused on the even point like 30-30 and deuces. If those points are won, that will set you up and give you the confidence to win the game; if not, no harm done, but you will need to work your way back to deuce.
- If opponent is stronger than you, play focused on 15-30 down, so if you get the next point you can feel you are back in the game.

All Sets
- Always win the 1st game (early lead).
- If opponent is not strong focus on the 7th game (middle): 3-3$\rightarrow$ 4-3 $\rightarrow$ *lead* (then, hold your serving game and you will lead 5-3).
- If opponent is about your level focus at 4-4, 5-5. By winning the following game, you are just one step away from the set (and a significant psycologycal advantage).
- Always concentrate on the last game. Sometimes it is hard to close out the set (or match).
    - Do not change a winning plan. Use the strategy that let you win all those games.

- Maximize your strength and increase margins for error (use more topspin, and aim well inside the lines), but keep dictating the point.
- Make sure your mind does not wander. Keep your mind on the task at hand, based on a solid, sound strategy, and you will stay relaxed and play in the "zone."

Second Set
- Be aware of momentum shifts (if your opponent wins 2 or 3 points in a row, a momentum shift can be created).
- If you won the first set, do not lose your momentum by letting your opponent somehow come back (usually carelessness after winning the first set). Instead, keep dictating your game and adapt to countering any changes in your opponent's strategy (do not forget he wants this set badly after losing the first).
- If you lost the first set, look for an opportunity during the first games of the second set (usually when your opponent relaxes or plays a lazy- loose point). By getting an early lead in the second set, you have a greater chance to take the set.

Tiebreak (12 Point Tiebreaker)
- Get an early lead by dictating your game based on the plan that let you win most of the points, taking also into consideration that a tiebreak requires a solid first serve.
- Playing focused at 5-3 up or down will determine a victory or a comeback.

IF LOSING THE MATCH (during changeovers)
- Analyze the situation (identify the problem) and be flexible to adapt (change tactics or plans).
- *Change Pace*
  - If opponent is hitting aggressively (match is progressing too fast), slow down with floaters (moon-shots) or drop shots.
  - If opponent hits slow pace shots, moon-balls, or inconsistently, attack with volleys, or aggressive shots.[1]
- Aim *deep* with heavy topspin to the center of the court to minimize unforced errors.
- Concentrate on *not losing more than two points in a row*. Once you lose more than two points, your opponent will gain a high level of confidence. By the same token, if you lose two points in a row, try to *neutralize* your opponent with an effective strategy.

- Against a better player, never try to play beyond your limits (over-hitting shots). Play your game while focusing on consistency and percentage.
- Pay attention to your opponent's physical fitness. If you lost the first set, but your opponent is wearing out, keep hitting to the open court, use drop shots and lob him to deplete his energy, and you will have control over the second set.
- Always look for a solution to the situation. The easier way is by asking yourself questions about what you are doing and what your opponent is doing. In other words, you need to find out what your opponent's strategy is, and where he is successful. What is your strategy, and where are you failing? Without knowing this information you will not have too many chances to turn the game in your favor.
- Identify momentum shifts as early as possible. These shifts can happen as you or your opponent win a couple of points in a row, as couples of games are won consecutively, or if one set is won.
- Always drink fluids and, if you get hungry, have a bite of banana, a bagel, a pretzel, or a power bar.

IF LOSING THE RHYTHM

- Keep footwork as a priority (move your feet, keep them active).
- On backcourt rallies split step twice. First, split when the ball bounces at the opponent's side and the second before his point of contact.
- Make sure you get ready to strike the ball (racquet back, get behind the ball) before the ball bounces on your side.
- Make sure you are using all the body links in the right order of execution (sequence, coordination).[3]
- Focus only on the ball and the present point (beware of distractions).
- Impose your game and your strength, disregarding your opponent.
- Play high percentage tennis, using more topspin and not going for the lines.[2]
- Keep a competitive attitude (never give up) at all times, especially when off rhythm.
- Some players will use excessive talk as a tactic to slow down the game or repetitive shoelace tying. They might towel off after each point, taking too much time between points (sometimes the opposite), or make bad calls (honest mistakes and deliberately bad calls). Make sure when any of this happens, you stay focused on your game and strategy, and you keep footwork active (move or skip in place). Never get upset about bad calls. Complain and show that you disagree, and then accept that in every match there will be a certain number of bad calls against you, but that won't make you lose the match.

IF LOSING CONCENTRATION

- Keep your mind in the present time. Do not watch spectators or engage in a conversation with anybody but yourself.
- Use relaxation techniques (see below, "Controlling Anxiety") to stay in or regain the present moment.
- Keep emotions in check (do not get too excited when making a great shot, and do not lament when you make a mistake).
- Do not let a mistake get in your way of winning the following point. Forget about it and move on to the next point.
- Exert extreme effort on every point.
- *Signs of Lack of Concentration*
  - Too many unforced errors (losing games too quickly).
  - Continuously losing track of the score.
  - Thinking of other tasks or issues rather than the present moment.
- *Focus on the Ball* (Eyes Control)
  - Watch the ball leaving your racquet, follow its flight across the net to your opponent's racquet, and follow its way back to you. Continue focusing on the ball in this conscious manner until the point is over.
  - At high-speed tennis, when the ball moves too fast, *focus on the ball when it gets to the peak of the bounce* before you and your opponent makes contact (the ball bounces up, **stops**, and then starts to come down). It is easy to visualize it when it stops.
  - Watch the ball rotation (try to realize its spin).
  - Try to see the seams of the ball, especially at the peak of its bounce.
  - Focus on the bounce of the ball and point of contact by saying at the perfect timing **"bounce"** (when ball bounces on your side)—**"hit"** (when you make contact).

- Know **Your** *Ideal Point of Contact Area* (Striking Zone)

Groundstrokes

> Point of contact is found around waist level, out in front, and on the side of the body.

Volley

> Point of contact is found ideally at eye level, aligned with the front shoulder, and on the side of the body.

Serve / Overhead

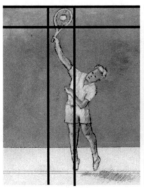 

> Point of contact is found high at full stretch, out in front, and on the side of the body.

- To find your point of contact use a grid to consistently meet the ball in the right spot (in space), disregarding spin, speed or placement (running shots) of the ball.
- At high level tennis, when watching the ball at the peak of the bounce is already in the system, and the ball moves at high speed, use the grid technique to focus on the ball without stressing your eyes. Eyes are like camera lenses. When the ball is on the other side at opponent's racquet, your eye focus is in long distance vision. As the ball approaches you, at your point of contact, your eye focus is in short distance vision. Focusing on the ideal point of contact area *before* you make contact, instead of focusing *only* on the ball, will relax you and force you to move better in order to meet the ball in that specific area and, therefore, to play automatic tennis (in the "zone").
- In order to have consistency on all of your strokes (reducing unforced errors) and, at the same time, maintain concentration throughout the point, imagine the grid while hitting the ball. Recognize when you are making contact outside the ideal striking zone grid (especially behind or late).

CONTROLLING ANXIETY

- Do not force yourself to play extremely hard. Work hard on the court (especially footwork), but let it happen. Trying extremely hard will only tighten up your muscles, wearing you out prematurely and slowing you down. Consequently, you will under perform (high muscle tension on the arm will lead to reduced wrist motion and decrease of spin, as well as reduced blood flow and decrease of feel, leading to over-hitting or pushing the ball. Tension in the legs will cause a reduced range of motion, slowing down the effectiveness of your footwork. Mental tension will impair your ability to focus, as well as decrease eye vision sharpness, critically necessary for quick reactions).
- When feeling tight, shake hands, shoulders, or do some neck rotation.
- Try to enjoy, even if the match is not going well (take the hard times with a smile).
- Try to relax at changeovers. If anxiety is high, divert your thoughts from the match. Relax, and you will play better.
- Do several deep breaths (inhaling from the nose, exhaling from the mouth).
- Breathe out when hitting the ball.
- Think only of the present point.
- Think performance over outcome. Always put out 100% effort, and this way anxiety will drop because you are not focusing on the result.

- Believe in yourself and think positively.
- Do not underestimate or overestimate your opponent. Just map your strategy and execute it accordingly. Remember: play the ball, not the opponent.
- Do not be a perfectionist. Let yourself make some mistakes, especially when your opponent hits forcing shots (which differ from your own unforced errors).
- Always move fast (reaction/footwork), but don't rush into hitting the shot (controlling physical anxiety). First, get early in position to hit it and then have a control shot (smooth upper body). Also, as you prepare or hit the ball, do not think what kind of shot you are hitting or about to hit, neither change your mind on any particular shot, during or just before execution (controlling mental anxiety).

Note: Most of the ideas and tips shown in this chapter must to be well practiced before you put them into action, so when you play your match that new information gets incorporated in your game, and, therefore, you can play in the "zone" (automatic tennis).

[1] See chapter "**Different Players**"
[2] See chapter "**Strategy**"
[3] See *Kinetic Body Chain* in book 1, chapter "**Stances**"

AFTER THE MATCH

AFTER THE MATCH

COOL DOWN

- Stretching while muscles are warm may reduce the risk of injury (increasing range of motion), therefore, always stretch after a workout (cool down).[1]
- Fluid replacement. An adult can lose about 2.5 liters of sweat per hour on a hot day match.
- Eat high-glycemic carbohydrates (allows muscles to recover after exercise) like corn flakes, oatmeal, potatoes, honey, rice cakes, raisins, bagels and breads. Also, some fruits like bananas and oranges are good choices.

Stretching

- Hold the stretch between 20 to 40 seconds.
- Avoid bouncing movements.
- Stretch slowly up to the point of tightness.
- Never feel pain while stretching.
- Focus on staying relaxed (throughout the stretch) while breathing normally.

- **Forearm Stretch**
  Extend arms forward in front of the body. First, pull the palm up with the other hand. After that, push palm down. Repeat stretch with the other arm.

- **Shoulder Stretch**
  A. Put one arm across the chest, and with the other arm push from elbow towards the chest. Repeat stretch with the other arm.

B. With one arm over and behind the head and the other under and behind the back, try to make both hands meet together (behind back). It can be facilitated with a towel or a racquet. Repeat stretch with the other arm.

- **Hip Stretch**
  Standing with feet shoulder width apart, hold one arm by the elbow behind the head and pull to the side. Switch arms and pull to the other side.

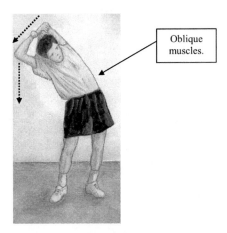

Oblique muscles.

- **Back and Hamstring Stretch**
  Standing with legs straight and feet close together, touch toes with fingertips or as far as possible.

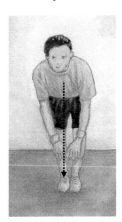

Variations

Feet shoulder
width apart.
Hands to toes.

- **Back, Shoulder, and Hamstring Stretch**
  With hands behind the back interlocked, pull upward as your head pushes downward.

Hamstring
muscles.

- **Groin Stretch**
  Stand with feet wide spread apart. With hands together, bend one knee as far as you can go. The head stays up and body faces forward throughout the stretch. Repeat stretch with the other leg.

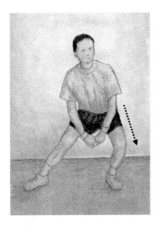

- **Quadriceps Stretch**
  Standing on one leg, hold ankle and pull it to the buttocks. Switch legs.

Quadriceps muscles.

93

- **Calf Stretch**

  Standing straight, facing sideways with the feet widely spread apart, lower your weight down, closing the gap between the back heel and the floor. Repeat stretch with the other leg.

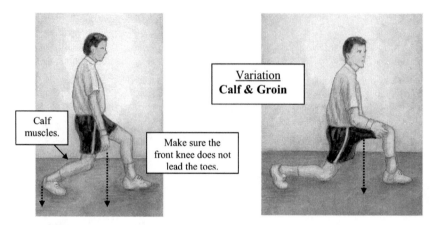

Variation
Calf & Groin

Calf muscles.

Make sure the front knee does not lead the toes.

- **Knee Flexion**

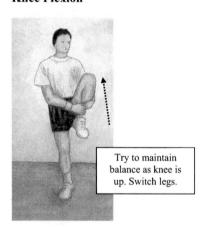

Try to maintain balance as knee is up. Switch legs.

Variation

- **Knee & Spine Flexion**

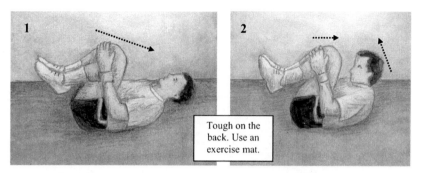

Tough on the back. Use an exercise mat.

- **Hamstring Stretch**
  Sit on the floor with one leg extended forward and other leg bent inward. The knee should touch the floor. Lean chest forward to the extended leg as far as you can (hands grab the extended foot if possible). Switch legs.

- **Hamstring and Groin Stretch**
  On the floor with legs apart as far as possible, bend from the hip, and try to grab your toes.

- **Lower Back Stretch**
  A. Back Twist
  Sitting on the floor, cross one leg over the other, keeping the knee high (on the crossed leg). Twist back with both arms toward the opposite side of the crossed leg. Switch legs and reverse the stretch.

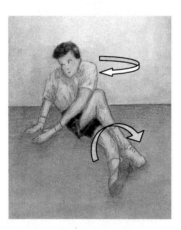

B. Spine Twist

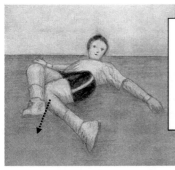

Lying on the floor, cross legs and twist to the opposite side of the crossed top leg (bottom knee to the floor). Concentrate on keeping the shoulders and hips flat on the floor. Switch legs and reverse twist to the other side.

Variations

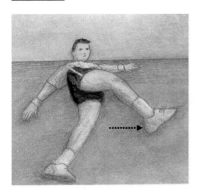

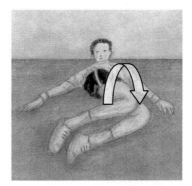

- **Spine Flexion**

Push head upward as back is pulled down.

Push head downward as back is pulled up.

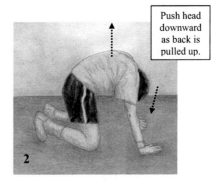

Variation

- **Spinal Flexion & Forearm Stretch**

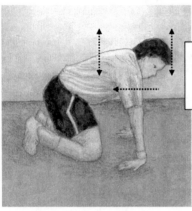

With fingers facing towards you, pull your body backward, flexing the spine (use previous stretch technique for spinal flexion).

- **Inner Thigh Stretch**
  Sitting on the floor, hold the feet together close to the groin. Lean trunk forward as far as you can go, trying to keep the knees close to the floor.

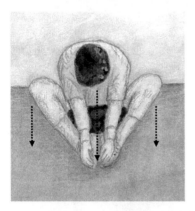

AVOIDING INJURIES

Causes of Injuries

- Poor Technique[2]
  The major goal for any successful tennis player is to have biomechanically sound strokes, not only to play efficiently, but to avoid injury. The basis of biomechanical strokes is to minimize the use of weak muscles, like the forearm (tennis elbow), as well as maximize the use of large group of muscles, like the quadriceps (legs), trunk, and shoulders. These large muscles, used with proper technique, will generate ground forces, which eventually will be the main power transferred into the ball. Also, biomechanically sound strokes facilitate the use of the body links (kinetic body chain) which, together with the ground forces, make stroke production effortless.

- Improper Exercise/Rest Ratio
  Most of the time in any anaerobic training, like tennis, the work/rest ratio should be 1/3. If proper rest time is not enforced, performance will decline, and the risk of injury will be greater.

- Over-training or Abusive Use of Particular Muscles
  Over-training can lead to burnout (physical and mental exhaustion, loss of joy for the game), and any extreme use of particular muscles, without adequate strength training, can lead to injury.

- Age and Capability of Level of Training
  The level of adequate training (conditioning aerobic and anaerobic, flexibility, agility, and strength training) should be determined by a professional, according to your age and overall fitness.[1]

- Inadequate Warm Up Before Extensive Training
  Tennis players perform constant movements, which include sprints, lateral shuffles, jumps, crossovers, and, unlike other sports, tennis requires the whole body for stroke production. Muscles are like rubber bands, when cold and stretched, they may break. Therefore, playing without proper warm up can lead to injury.[3]

LEARNING FROM MISTAKES

Analyzing the Match

The learning process starts by recognizing mistakes and weak spots that your opponent can exploit. After every match, analyze or have somebody charting where the majority of unforced errors occurred. Also, find out what kind of game style you played. Did you follow through with your preset plans? Did you attack the short balls? Did you make forcing shots? Did you find your opponent's weaknesses and exploit them? If you lost your rhythm, did you try to get it back? These are some of the questions that you should be asking yourself after the match.

As for the mental part, did you get nervous? How did you control anxiety? Did you get upset with yourself after a mistake? How was your focus and concentration? Did you have fun (even if you lost the match)? Did you learn something from the match or from your opponent (do not underestimate your opponent)? These are just some questions that you should ask yourself after every match (win or lose). Come up with your own set of questions, and you will see how productive every match will be.

Charting Future Goals

Once you have an idea of what the major problems are in your game or which areas need improvement, write them down as goals to be achieved with specific target dates. You could write short-term goals for something that you want to happen in the next 4-6 months or long-term goals for longer than that. Make sure that these goals are based on performance (physical and mental skills), not outcomes (consequences of performance), and that they are realistic and reachable.

Keeping a goal sheet active and updated will force you to attack and follow a strategy to solve those weak spots of which your opponent always seems to take advantage.

[1] Before engaging into a routine, seek advice from a qualified specialist.
[2] Always consult a professional about proper technique (biomechanically sound strokes). Playing tennis with poor technique can lead to injury.
[3] See chapter **"Before the Match"**

CPSIA information can be obtained at www.ICGtesting.com
Printed in the USA
269125BV00006B/317/P

9 781604 940510